Unposted Letters

Donald W. Baker

First Printing

ISBN 0-935306-23-4
Library of Congress Catalog Card Number 83-73208

Some of the poems in this book first appeared in
College English, *Green River Review*, *Laurel
Review*, *The Minnesota Review*, *New Letters*,
Poetry, *The Wabash Review*, and *The Windless
Orchard*.

Publication of this book was assisted by a grant
from the Indiana Arts Commission.

Graphics by Barbara LaRue King.

The Barnwood Press Cooperative
RR 2 Box 11C
Daleville, IN 47334

Printed in The United States of America.

Again to Natalie, Pamela, and Alison

Contents

IV   Unposted Letters

Part I   The Fire-Bearers

Sunrise

This is a morning that sings us
a child's rhyme, full of shining eyes.

The shadows of the leaves flutter
with the soft breathing of the sea.

If you walked naked over the meadow
among the cobwebs, the bees, and the wild roses,

all those you love would come
and walk with you and bless the earth.

Piano Sonata

The end of a journey,
listening here,
tears in my eyes:
that other country,
twelve generations,
ivory by candlelight:
and at sunrise
the green mountainside
in clear air,
the sheep so high
they seem white stones.

The Opening

Here is the sculptor.
A drop of burgundy glistens on his moustache.
There is his wife,
who has made him put on a jacket and tie.
The touches of wine in their eyes
urge you on, into the gallery,
sipping, looking.
You journey from spotlight to spotlight.
The pieces unfold
into planes of darkness,
pillars of light.
A cone of aluminum quivers,
a pyramid shakes,
spaces between them open like doors.
When you pause,
lifting your glass,
you notice the blue pulse in your wrist,
the white half-moon in your thumbnail.
Now you can name it,
this world,
its flames and powers:
Star,
Breaking Sea,
Woman of Fire.

The Concert

1   The Flute

Walking home, after the concert,
the flute, the viola still filling
our heads, we pass the maples
beyond the chapel, suddenly
step into sunlight, yes, April
at last, clouds thinning eastward,
sycamores, redbuds gleaming
with rain. It's Sunday, the campus
almost deserted, cardinals echoing
flutesong, and you, smiling, humming
the Mozart, taking my hand
like a girl again. Remember
the April after the war, Waterman
Street, the basement apartment,
sun through the window an hour
a morning, at night the candles,
bookshelves of orange crates,
Deborah giggling, Charles reading
Cleland aloud, our poems, music,
the kissing, all of us drunk,
still alive, still alive, still alive.

2   The Gallery

The flute lighted the gallery,
too, Gregory's paintings, Lillian's
sculpture, told us of heirlooms,
periwigs and before, 3,000 years,
a child, naked, flashing
through pasture into a grove.
I heard green water, then,
beyond the rocks, the sun
suspended over the mountains,
showering down, burning my
shoulders. Imagination,
they say, is a pattern of cells,
but who are these dead, living
within us? I closed my eyes,
and the flute wandered 10,000
lives, took my hand like a lover,
a muse, through that frozen city,
the rooms of my childhood, full
of uncles and snow, the voices
of mother, summer, photographs
on the walls, lighting up
there in the kitchen, geranium,
skillet, a pipe in an ash tray.
Then the sun through the window,
saying my name, touching my shoulder,
a flute in a gallery, music
like rain. Then it was you, breath
warm on my cheek as you whispered.

3   The Poem

Piano   cello   viola   flute
the bow, the breath, tracing the hour,
the intricate way, seeking
the eye of the maze, the midnight
chord, where the pattern concludes
itself. We listened to paintings,
too, the clouded windows, blue
to the lakes, green to the prairies
of Indiana. No. These words
are wrong, I can't make the poem, I
make the noises of vanity, hunger,
assembling syllables, fitting
the phrases together. I nail up
crude signs under the paintings.
Do me a favor: tell me I'm naked,
tell me to crawl from this page.
Then the flute plunged like a diver,
the piano glittered like bees
on the walls, the cello soared,
the viola exploded, we sat
in a flight of feathery chords
that hovered around us. You understand,
I am trying to piece it together,
the broken faces, the scattered
music, trying to place
our moment, our poem, perfect
as noon, in the palm of your mind.

Language

I no longer trust words
                    —Lillian Hellman

Whatever the words say,
it is the hand touching the arm that matters,
the apple peeled and shared.

But we are not born dumb.
Something in us urges another proof,
by color, clay, sound, movement, even

language, even the words you mistrust,
the words that allow themselves
to be stolen, sold, caged, exhibited, possessed,

but that sometimes, perhaps
in the dark on a sweaty pillow,
on some page, in some phrase you remember,

touch each other
as a woman and a man touch,
put for good the tang of apple on the tongue.

Essential Questions

My job is to get up in the morning
and start writing poems.
It's at least as useful
as getting up in the morning
and starting to sell Cap'n Crunch.
I put on my jeans and sneakers,
eat two eggs over and a bran muffin,
and sit down at the living room window
with a cup of tea.

Vic Sammartino drives by
on his way to work.
He waves.
His busy smile expresses superiority and disdain,
because he thinks I am doing nothing.
He reminds me of the chairman of my department,
who prefers publishing scholars.
He'd better be careful.
Look what happened when they called Hitler
a lazy slob.

Meanwhile, I rake my imagination
for something to write about.
Am I an alcoholic?
Will my kidneys last out the year?
Are these the essential questions?
Are they fit subject for poetry?
What *is* fit subject for poetry?
How can I tell?
Do I care?
So one inspiration leads to another
down the labyrinthine ways
of the poet's mind.

Mike Donovan's daughter walks by,
off to the municipal pool,

in what appears to be a bikini.
She doesn't wave.
No doubt her illiterate father
has poisoned her mind against poets.
She reminds me of high school summers,
girls named "Priscilla" and "Leona,"
who float on my mind's eye
like rubber dolls in a bathtub.

Perhaps I should have been Gaius Valerius Catullus,
lounging at poolside,
composing a poem for Patty Donovan,
"voluptuous virgin," phrases like that.
In Latin.
It's no good.
If my wife ever had it translated,
she'd kill me.

Bradford Dunbar goes by, the corporate lawyer,
jogging.
He pretends to look at his watch,
then runs as hard as he can to intimidate me.
He thinks I'm a failure
and out of shape.
OK, Dunbar, I know you saw me.
Lickspittle capitalist lackey!
He sprints to catch up with Donovan's daughter,
who blows him a kiss
as he passes.
They don't fool me.
He's not her uncle.

Maybe I should have been Pablo Neruda,
hiding out in the Rockies,
writing a political poem,
"Letter from the Extreme Left,"
that would sweep the country.
I see Reagan, Haig, and Bradford Dunbar,
in Adidas and jogging shorts,
fleeing to Argentina.

They are arrested by Cuban police.
Poets wreck all the nuclear energy plants,
and I win the Nobel Prize.

So that's that.
What more can one do in a morning?
I get up with my notes,
go into my study,
and sit down at my typewriter.
It needs a new ribbon.
Well, it always takes a few days
to think through and polish a poem.
It's twenty after eleven.
Let's call it noon.
Let's mix a martini,
and contemplate politics, love,
and the essential questions.

Fire-Bearers

At dusk the fireflies appear,
here, there, rising from hollows
in the grass. As night gathers,
hundreds gleam and go out.

They stir me more than stars,
those permanent bombs, blindly
glittering, riddling our flesh
through blasted girders of the pines.

Glimpses of pure light, these
fire-bearers, coldly passionate,
shining from hollow places,
seeking each other in the dark.

Part II   Walking Sideways

Walking Sideways

For several years now
I've been walking sideways.
That way I don't have to see
where I'm going or where I've been.
It's made me comfortable.
I don't need to go to church any more.
I don't chew my nails.
Yesterday, on Washington Street,
I noticed a woman doing the same thing:
long smooth slides,
my kind of sidle.
Then she disappeared in the crowd.
But I know now
there are at least two of us.
So I'm working up a petition,
soliciting signatures.
If they make it legal,
I'll advertise.

Drinking Alone

At six,
sitting next to me at the bar,
I notice myself,
lifting a highball.

He is eying me, too,
equally startled,
suspicious.

At seven,
one on each side of us,
you appear,
leggy as ever,
sipping a gimlet.

Darling,
the four of us,
years rinsed out
like dregs from a glass,
a glittering evening again.
We dance,
play musical barstools,
kiss,
pretend there are marriages going on.

At eight,
as usual,
one of us speaks,
accusation
poised on an eyelid.

You put down your glass,
step back again
carefully into yourself,
smile,

and go.

That door has closed
hundreds of times.

And at nine,
not letting me notice,
I slip back again
too, into one
on a single stool,

lifting a glass
to a sidelong moment,
undoubled again,
and again.

Recital

Stunned by the consecrated frown of this child,
whose fingers stumble over keys, pelting
the room with showers of tinkling tone,
whose bright braids sway and whose mouth is fruited
and who, glowing in a pink frock, curtseys:
cushioned and cool I breathe in silver water,
melt in the center of sunlight.

Over seaweed lace on the shore of a cape
a gull once caught me with flashes, gliding,
and lay stark white upon the water; and a black fin
like a looting blade slashed the sea
and the gull vanished with splashing.

Now, regardless of grandeur, bellowing
mongrels drag down a fawn in my forest,
and I, heartless in glutting my hungers,
have shuddered in an eclipse of the sun.
Damp, hot, black in my ultimate and earthy cave,
I dream: myself those dogs, that dark.

Psychopathia Sexualis

I fall in love quite easily now
with the plants,
the squash, for instance,
sweet, yellow G-clefs
crooning to elephants' ears
on the sunny side of the house,
or the tomatoes, red eyeballs
peering from ferny sockets.
To say nothing of indoor passions:
my wife little suspects
that I get up at midnight
to stroke the polished skin
of her philodendron.
This seems in part
the fruit of tedium and satiety.
I have known thirty-two women,
not many according to Casanova,
but enough to comprise
an adequate random sample.
If you pluck another,
the rose does not screech its jealousy
at you at three in the morning.
If you walk out of the garden,
the hydrangea goes right on blooming.

A psychiatrist friend, who told me
professors were especially subject
to quaint perversions,
confessed that (to test a theory, he said)
he once made love to a tree,
a young birch, I recall,
in a woodsy vale in Vermont.
He praised the pale sheen of its bark,
the willowy wood of its trunk,
and said that there in the shadows

under the stars, leaves trembling,
branches yielding around him,
he felt love as he'd never felt it before.
Then he asked me to confide.
He's never married, that doctor.
And I have given up scholarship
and spend much of my life
leafing through garden books.

Next spring I think I shall plant
morning glories,
those enticing vines hung
with huge Tyrian blooms
that open and close with the day.
Imagine, at dawn,
caught up in their stems and tendrils,
kissing them bud after bud
till they break into blossom.
As a fallen professor I say,
besides the psychosexual truth,
there's an old moral lesson
in these revelations:
you must know yourself;
you must come to choose not merely
your residence and profession.

Naked Daughter

Under your skin, daughter,
blue veins map the rivers of Europe,
my Clyde, my Shannon,
your mother's Elbe, Dniester,
mixed in your blood, daughter,
our tribes, Celts, Saxons,
women in fleece, fire-makers,
washers on stones at the river bank.

And there, among a thousand blondes,
that palm, that orchard of pomegranates,
there in the high bone of your cheek,
your eyes almost aslant,
she, Natalia Rebecca,
Ashkenazi, rabbi's daughter,
child singing in the shtetl.

What blemish is her token?
That mole? That crooked tooth?
Remember stubbing your toe in Odessa?
Blood splashed in the Ukrainian dust?
Babi Yar, Treblinka—
all those fathers and daughters—
and she whose blood you share,
your dark cousin, living here,
in the blue rivers
flowing to your heart.

Part III   Delinquent Elegies

The Technical Imperative

No camps, no ovens,
nothing as crude
as botulism or firestorm.

You understand:
clean ruins
and no survivors.

A clenched glove
with a hand in it
laid on a desk.

American Summer

It was my daughter
lost at nine years old
huddled in the cellar
behind the lawn mower
and the coiled hose
her eyes shut tight
her frail hands
stopping her ears.
"It's over now.
"It's all over," I said.
But when I stooped
to lift her up
the windows flashed
the walls tottered
the explosions
knocked us down
choking in the dust.
Her mouth swooned
without a sound
her eyes fled
she kicked out of my arms
like a hurt cricket
scuttled into a corner
tried to squeeze herself
into the watering can.
"Don't be crazy.
"They won't hurt us," I said.
But it was a long time
before she would listen
to her tenth year
and I could take her hand
and lead her up
past the smoking webs
draped over the wheelbarrow

up into the garden
to enjoy the silver bees
the bursting pods
the roseflames
of American summer.

The Metropolitan Area

The base camp of the expedition
that white tent in the clearing. At night
we shivered in mists from the river. Things
shook the brush beyond the fire-circle.

In daylight, snapshots:
here, old cables rusting into rock
seared by a couple of blasts;
there, a crushed rib cage under giant
ferns; bones around a broken axe.

The poet of the party had some luck:
that squirrel climbing a dead oak;
those sparrows; and that starving cat.

Then we saw this woodcarver, squatting
near a den in the riverbank, making music.
He had whittled a willow whistle
and danced around the skeleton of a child.
We had to shoot him.

Delinquent Elegies

for Keith Douglas (1920-1944)

John Smith (1923-1944)

My friend John Smith, a usual man,
urging his bomber from the earth,
heard his life end in a loud bang
and took fire with his last breath.

Our engines idled through the necessary pause,
until his passion was extinguished.
Then the others of the squadron rose
into the morning, over John Smith's ashes,

bombed, and at noon returned, most of them,
to the hut where, with one dropping eye,
the colonel drew the obvious lesson:
how not to fly.

No day could have been more ordinary.
So much was burning in that bad time
that no one troubled to sing an elegy
for John Smith and his crew of nine.

That was almost forty years ago.
Now in the evening on our TV
the shining bombers climb and show
us how it was, is, and again will be,

while here, where only a desk lamp burns,
I rake old anguish to make my truth
and record at last some ordinary rhymes,
a late song for a long-dead youth,

my friend John Smith, who, in the Second War,
blew up and burned, one among many,
a clownish hero, killed by error,
as smart as most, as brave as any.

Ed Jones (1922-1944)

Ed Jones from Alabama,
a tall lieutenant in O'Connor's crew,
with an unpleasant *smack* stepped into a propeller.
No one could tell us whether he'd
stumbled or simply had enough of flak and fighters.
No matter: most of his head lay puddled
at one end of a sudden corpse
in fleece and leather,
and nevermore would Jones the navigator
level a bubble-octant at a star.

We died by hundreds,
burnt over Schweinfurt, ditched in the North Atlantic,
reduced to a DFC,
a packet of letters in a drawer at home,
no less ignominiously scared or despairing,
nineteen or twenty-two,
than Jones, who sprawled in brains and gristle,
flat on the flight line behind the BOQ,
in a bloody dawn framed in a gray scud,
a young man some disliked, some loved.

Here, now, Jones hangs abstract,
delight and horror dreamed in flamboyant line,
sun-red, fog-gray, blood-black,
recollected, reconstructed,
sheer design,
a galleried geometry of tongue and breath—
an instance, madam, for your delectation,
of the "supreme fiction,"

the end of things,
the paradoxical apocalypse of poetry:

a banal transformation, breath to death:
a Tuscaloosan drawl, long fingers holding a heart flush,
blind hungers that flew, fucked, and got drunk
the way we all did (the Blue Moon in Algiers)—
abruptly spilled;
and wondrous metamorphosis,
a winged image that lets down gently now
through icy years, and taxis into line, and cuts the engines,
here, where Jones continually collapses,
crushed and beautiful.

Bill Williams (b. 1922)

Bill Williams, bombardier,
flew once and disappeared,
not on a mission,
but in the middle of the night.
Major Grimes said nothing
but looked grim,
breaking Bill's replacement in.
The joke among the crews
was D.O.F.—
Died (not of Flight) of Fright.
But some of us suspected
Bill was less scared than wise:
Dortmund, Kassel, Schweinfurt
lay ahead,
and those guys
in the Focke-Wulfs,
defending their own skies,
were too much, even for the Major—
who burned heroically
with all his crew
one cloudless morning
over Regensburg.
Bill Williams would be sixty, now,

my age,
is probably alive somewhere,
grandfather, suburbanite,
respected lawyer—who knows,
mayor.
George Grimes is still the Major,
still a hero,
still twenty-eight,
still dead.
Bill Williams, as I said,
flew once
and woke up early.
The rest of us
woke when we died—
or twenty, thirty years later,
half-comprehending what we did.

The Coffin

"all a poet can do today is warn"
—Wilfred Owen

There's no use writing this poem.
It will be bad.
It will stay unpublished and unknown,
except that, as usual, I shall read it
to my wife and a few friends.
I think of them on their feet,
clapping and whistling,
swearing never to join the Marines again.
For this is a poem written by me against war,
and that is how wife and friends ought to react,
accepting the artifact for the achievement,
ego for truth.
Actually, little remains to be said against war.
It's foolish, trying to add
argument, anecdote, or emotion
to what better poets than I
have already written.
And those among you not Nazis at heart
have no need to be told.
But by way of parenthesis,
in this dissertation on bad poetry,
let me give it the ring of the lecture hall,
let me make a statement of theme:
Nothing is worse than a war.
Pause, for wife and friends to applaud. . . .
Thank you.
Yes, that's what this poem insists,
that nothing is worse than a war,
though I have been repeatedly and excitedly warned,
by professors and other experts,

that polemic stultifies art:
metrical brilliance, architectonical genius—
irrelevant, once your poem engages itself.
Too bad.
These are ripe times
for poems that speak against war.
I should have enjoyed annoying them all
by composing a good one.
You've probably noted the virtuosity
posturing vainly in back of this discourse.
Lines 10, 11, and 12, for instance,
quintuple vowel alliteration, triple internal rhyme,
and the whole poem,
with small neglect of intelligence,
a *tour de force*,
practically purged of metaphor—
except in that word "purged"
and one or two others, "ripe," line 35 above.
Ah, me!
The craft so long to lerne,
wasting itself on a poem so *engagé*.
Dear wife, dear friend, dear reader:
this poem, already too long,
raises, like war, a tough technical problem:
how, successful or not, to stop it.
A last line should click into place,
someone has said, like the lid of a coffin.
But there's no point in wasting technique
on a poem dead from the start.
So I'll let you end it, dear people.
Abandon your minds, for once, to imagination.
Imagine I've stopped.
Imagine I'm stepping aside
to let the professors rise and rebut.
Many things, they will tell you, including this poem,
are worse than a war.
And who knows?
We're all rational, liberal here.
They may be right.

But now, before hearing them,
why don't you test your technical skill?
Ready?
Begin.
Imagine the coffin.
Imagine the lid.
Imagine the click.

Part IV   Unposted Letters

Unposted Letter

Fall is my best season, summer
settled like dust, everything
neatly in place in good time.
A fresh start, as they say, as if
I had you to look forward to,
leaves falling, Swope Park, 1943.
Thirty-five years. When I left,
you called in sick, a Thursday,
I think it was, Union Station,
Track 7, 10:40 a.m. I gave you
my silver wings. Summer of
Schweinfurt, Regensburg.
Four of my friends shot down.
You know how it is, days, nights
adding up, human frailty, other
easy excuses. Life is one long
betrayal. Said he. Now history
is cheerful as ever, this fall they
are scrutinizing again the west
bank of the Jordan, Jack's brains
splashed on her hands. My summer
was placid and short. I am happy,
on leave from my college, more honestly
loving my wife. My daughters
are women. I write very
few letters. I don't know why
I must tell you all this.

The Prize

My daughter drives from Northampton
to spend a few days with me and my wife.
On Monday, the sun blazing,
we walk the flats at low tide.
She talks about Walter, her husband,
their new washing machine, their ambitions.
On Tuesday we lunch in the Red Inn at Provincetown,
quahog pie, Indian pudding.
How cool she is!
After thirty years our child is gone.
On Wednesday night at the cottage
we see her slides of the wedding:
Beacon Street,
families and friends sipping champagne,
successful, superior in-laws.
I appear on the screen,
overexposed among those I love.
"How distinguished you look in your new suit!"
my wife exclaims, fighting back.
I do not look distinguished.
I am an aging professor, no waistcoat,
a bristly poet with pretentious beard.
My daughter, tactful as ever, switches the slides.
It's the groom's father, retired importer,
shorn, immaculate.
Rich.
I shrink back out of the light
and wish I were a distinguished poet.
Kunitz or Dugan, for instance,
living nearby, famous in P'town.
Kunitz, from Worcester, my old home town,
acquired a Pulitzer years ago.
So did Dugan, who's reading tonight in Truro.
I let ambition and envy
flush through my mind and gurgle away.
Who knows?

Maybe tomorrow I'll sit down to write
and succeed.
Be careful now, I'll say to myself.
Don't try too hard to make this a poem.
It begins at night, in your bed, you know,
in the salty mud of your mind,
a rhythm,
a barnacled hope,
heavy and cold as a quahog,
raked and pried out of bitterness.
In the morning it bleaches and blinds.
Simply and clearly phrases begin
to drop into place,
like slides in a carousel:
"quahog pie," "Indian pudding"
(a Pulitzer line if I ever made one).
Then, a matter of talent or luck,
they run out,
and you flounder, dumb,
through the whole afternoon,
among deliberations and blunders,
while in Boston, brick-red and gold,
behind brides and grooms,
among blossoms and sunlit wine,
unspeakable futures
are slouching towards you down Beacon Street.
Meanwhile, it's still Wednesday night.
I look back at the screen.
It's my daughter, the bride, with her bouquet,
her younger sister, slinky in lilac silk,
my wife, as usual, smoothing her hair.
The screen is alight and alive.
The poem is written.

A Bequest To My Daughter

Once, before dying, I hope
to say to you, daughter, what
no one can say. Trying, God knows,
I've strewn my life with cracked poems,
tossed here and there, now and then,
as easy as lying. The words keep
falling in clusters, never stop
failing. But what else can I use:
finger-paints? a player-piano?
I was born to this windy limbo.
Flabbergast yourself: close
the book of the foolish myth
you must read in my face, take
for once an uncluttered look:
mostly a comic life, in two
million acts, more or less, a mime
caught in disgraceful postures,
starving to speak, to justify,
being human. Then you might weep.
See? Even now I go round
and around. Listen, child:
Algiers, the white city, gone blue
in the blackout. Rickety table. Onions,
long bread, red wine. A candle. A bed.
A desert out there in the dark. . . .
Dakar. Seventy planes. Sunrise
like blood on the wings. Flame, black
smoke. My friend Paul Dickos dying
on fire in the African dust. . . .
Yes, I can draw you back, write
you exhausted fables, show
you far-wasted countries, spent
years, the ashen light that flickers
in whatever eloquence they evoke.
Still, I don't lie. Every failure

lifts some honest grief or joke
into view, makes me real, lets me
speak. I prayed with great poets
for beauty, courtesy for you,
helped you invent your childhood,
the barn in a shoebox, your white
terrier, the enormous starfish.
Now you have grown, gone out into our
century, violence, fanatical
beyond murder, beneath words,
pride that kills God. I cannot
know what door you have closed,
what wreck is burning behind you.
I speak half-dumbly here, a clown
diminishing, giving you legends,
a collection of loving words,
the lucky courage of poetry.
Yes, those at least I can offer, red
and black emblems, my own fearless
room in the desert, a loyal
column of smoke on the horizon.

The Metaphor

My wife and I give a party.
We invite a few of our old friends
and other professors and spouses.
They stand or sit in our living room,
drinking gin, while the stereo
plays old jazz. By a quarter to seven
the noise of voices begins to rise
and my wife is smiling.

I compliment George on a paper he's published.
I ask about Tony's children.
I joke with practically everyone.
Then I relax near the piano.
I talk a long time with Christina,
George's wife, with whom, years ago,
I shared a damn good affair.
Like George, she has slumped and fattened.
I see by her eyebrow she notes my new teeth.
But, when we turn from each other,
her knee teases mine, as it used to do,
and, drenched in the whiskey of lost love,
I remember her passionate whispers.

Later I see her chatting with Tony
and George in front of the picture window.
They laugh together and speak
with the easy gestures and touches of old friends.
The last light of September
is falling over their shoulders.
Their lifted glasses reflect the candles
that light, now, the table of *canapés*.
Suddenly a clarinet swings from the stereo,
and, in a glimpse like a snapshot,
they stop, stand without moving.
They seem fragile, balanced precariously.

How to say it now?
A kiss has ended?
The hands of a watch have frozen?
No.
The metaphor won't come quite right.
It may be I am not a poet.
But something conclusive has shortened my breath
and turned my friends to glass on a shelf.

Perhaps, after all, Christina, Tony, and George
are the perfect metaphor.
Perhaps they represent time perceptible,
as we all collapse into comical futures.
Perhaps this is the last party we shall ever give
at which, while I watch, my heart twenty years back,
Christina, Tony, and George
will stand together exactly like that,
drinking gin in a failing light.

Or perhaps that moment was not a poem,
only a pleasing noise,
drums and a clarinet out of 1940.

Look.
My wife is still coming and going,
not thinking my morbid thoughts.
Beneath her gray hair
her eyes shine with friendliness and amusement.
She warms our guests with her merry face.
When she passes, winking at me,
I must force myself not to reach for her hand.
I will not look again at the three at the window.
I am drunk enough to be happy and free of that future.
To hell with their poem.
To hell with its metaphor.
To hell with the meaning of life.

Evening

Suddenly it goes cold, night
coming up from the sea. All evening
we've talked, often in silence.
I've been an envious man, never
prizing my own, wanting that
better poem, that lovelier woman.
Now I envy children their
timeless hours, simple, like these.
When you lean towards me, the last light
stresses your eyes, those lines
at your mouth I've tried to lie
out of mirrors, write out of life.
That artifice makes its own
fear: that you live only in
me, in the dark behind closed
eyelids, the wish of my breath.
No more illusion. My poems
go ragged with age, moving only
with pain, all quieter, patient,
waiting for something else, now, not
the easy praise of the tongue.
Still, their grave compulsion goes
on, slides in like the flood.
I touch your fingers, the wind
gathers, rushes up from the cold
edge of the sea, the dark, year
after year. If we had twenty
more. Ten. To talk in silence,
keep telling more truth,
start loving again, knowing how.

The Catbird

This summer I have not yet written
one good poem.
I sit at this open window,
watching the catbird,
the crooked pines, and the slow
flame of the sun through the morning fog.
On quiet days I can hear the beat
of the sea on the shore beyond the dunes.
I drink tea,
and I wander back through the winters
as far as childhood.
I have even considered
believing in God.

Sometimes I sit for twenty minutes
and no word comes.
Or page after page taps itself
through my typewriter
and doesn't happen.
There are faces
I want to forget every day of my life,
cities
I no longer dare to remember.
It would be hard to persuade most people
that twenty seconds of typing in twenty minutes
is work.
It's certainly hard to persuade myself,
who was brought up to believe that work
was something exhausting you did for others,
who paid you a wage,
something, in fact, those others
could give and take when they wished.
I remember a winter a long time ago,
when burlap bags were heaped in the city hall,

and those who needed potatoes
could help themselves.
Outside it was snowing.
I try to write out of love and anger,
yet how banal the lines seem.

It's true, I no longer care a damn
for a pretty face,
and my wife and I have settled
into an easy routine.
If I were still political
and knew Spanish, I might write well
and furiously
and send letters south,
where corpses are scattered along the roads
and gunfire cracks out in the night.
Perhaps it is only old-fashioned despair,
perhaps it is cowardice,
that chooses the well-made phrase.

Or perhaps it is only the attempt
that matters.
Perhaps the poem begins and ends
where the sea beats,
at a depth where no strength of the imagination
can bring it forth.
Then the long strings of letters across the page
are a foolish vanity.
It is tempting to hope so.
For when it fails, then,
and I get up from my paper and turn away,
perhaps it becomes
the catbird,
perched for a moment
on the crooked bough of a pine,
quite black against the sudden sunlight.

Failure

I have one poem and one poem
only, no matter where it
begins, in anger, cigarette
smoke, it breaks out of absence,
solitude, hunts for a language,
a rhythm, turns, always,
inward, to you, where rivers
meet in that city. In those days
the taxi drove through the park,
the oaks in October, bronze
against blue, the lighted bridge
in the fog, how many journeys
away, now, young afternoons
behind drawn shades. The poem
speaks of those always, no matter
what words, what voice it discovers,
takes for its own, no matter how
far, how deeply it travels. Sometimes
it rages, bombing, over dead
farms, a city in ashes, sometimes
it shrinks into darkness, hungers
for silence. No matter who listens,
coward or lover, it speaks
of departure, darkening windows,
understands exile, loss, lies down
in fury, despair, turns, always,
inward, to you, to the intricate
ruins. Like remembered
dead, its face, when the mind
flares, never changes. Like love,
the poem, always a failure, prevails.

Donald W. Baker was born in Boston and educated by the Worcester public schools, Brown University, and the Army Air Corps. He is married to Natalie and is the father of Pamela and Alison. He is Milligan Professor of English Literature and Poet in Residence at Wabash College. His *Formal Application: Selected Poems, 1960-1980* also is available from Barnwood.